FOUR CLEVER BROTHERS

by Lynne Rickards

illustrated by Galia Bernstein

CAMBRIDGE
UNIVERSITY PRESS

UCL
Institute of Education

CAST LIST

The **Judge** is a wise man.
His name means 'justice'.

Gilad (a camel owner)
is a foolish man. His name
means 'camel's hump'.

The four brothers:

Tazim is the eldest brother
and his name means 'honour
and respect'. He is the natural
leader of the four, and his
brothers look up to him.

Kamran is a hard worker.
His name means 'successful'.

Sadiq is a serious young man.
His name means 'truthful'.

Latif is the youngest brother.
His name means 'kind'.

Judge: I am Adil the Judge. I am going to tell
you a story. It takes place in a dry
and dusty desert land.
My story concerns Gilad, the camel owner,
who came to me one hot afternoon
to settle an argument. This was
an unusual case, and I remember it well.
Everything I will tell you is true.

Judge: There once were four brothers, who were very good hunters. Their father taught them how to track an animal by listening and looking for clues on the ground. They learned everything about the way animals live and how they think. By the time the four brothers were adults, hunting came as naturally to them as breathing.

One day, the four brothers were walking along a path between two villages. The path was dry and sandy, with grass growing on each side. As they walked, the brothers spoke softly to each other.

Tazim: Do you see footprints on this path? Look, just here.

Kamran: It looks like something has passed this way recently.

Sadiq: They are smaller than the prints of a horse's hoof.

Latif: But they are spaced well apart. I would say it was a camel.

Tazim: Yes, that's just what I was thinking.

Judge: Suddenly, a man came rushing towards the four brothers, waving his arms in distress.

Gilad: Help! You, there! Please help me. Have you seen my camel? I'm sure someone has stolen it!

Judge: The four brothers looked at each other
with worried faces. Then they looked
at the camel owner.

Tazim: We would like to help you, sir.
Tell me, is your camel blind in one eye?

Gilad: Yes, it is!

Kamran: And is it lame in one foot?

Gilad: Yes, that is true too! It is an old camel,
and a bad-tempered beast,
but it's the only one I've got.

Sadiq: I'm sure we can help you find it.

Latif: Tracking animals is what we do best.

Gilad: *(to himself)* I am very pleased that the brothers seem to know my camel so well. But I wonder how that is possible.

Sadiq: I have another question for you, sir. Was your camel carrying a sack of wheat on one side?

Gilad: Indeed it was.

Latif: And did it have a jar of honey on the other side?

Gilad: That is exactly right! Come, come, you must think I am a fool. How do you know so much about my camel? You four men must have stolen my camel.

Tazim: No sir, we have not stolen your camel! Do we look like camel thieves?

Kamran: We have simply been walking along this path. I think you must have lost your camel somewhere else.

Sadiq: How could we have stolen it? A camel is too big to hide in a pocket! Feel free to search for yourself.

Latif: Believe us, sir. We have never even seen your camel!

Tazim: We have simply worked out what your camel is like from the many clues it left behind.

Gilad: What rubbish! I will have you arrested!

11

Judge: So Gilad had the four brothers arrested and brought to me.

Gilad: Adil, you are a man of justice. Hear my plea! These four men have stolen my camel and they must be punished. Will you help me?

Judge: Very well, Gilad. I will question them. What do you four men have to say for yourselves? How do you know so much about the missing camel?

Tazim: It is very simple, sir. I could tell the camel was blind in one eye because the grass was eaten only on one side of the path. Clearly, the camel did not see the grass on the other side.

Gilad: Humph. That is nonsense! How can he tell anything from a bit of grass?

Judge: Be patient, Gilad. We must hear all they have to say before making a judgement. Leave this to me.

Kamran: Sir, I knew the camel had one lame foot because of the prints it left in the sandy path. Three of its hoof prints were strong and clear, but one was not, because the camel couldn't put his weight on that foot.

Gilad: This man is trying to fool you, Judge. Don't believe him!

Judge: Gilad, you must let me decide. You have asked me to settle this argument, and you must let me consider all the facts. Please try not to interrupt.

Gilad: I'm sorry, Judge. Forgive me.

Judge: Now, what more can you four tell me? You, there.

Sadiq: Thank you, sir. I could tell that the camel was carrying a sack of wheat on one side very easily.

Judge: How was that? What clues did you see?

Sadiq: There was a trail of wheat grains on one side of the path, and the ants were gathering to carry it away. There must have been a hole in the sack of wheat that let the grains fall as the camel walked.

Judge: What about you, young man?
What do you have to say?

Latif: Sir, I saw drops of honey on the other side of the path. Flies were landing to taste the sweet honey. That is how I could tell the camel was carrying a pot of honey on the other side.

Gilad: What nonsense! How can a few ants or flies on a path tell you anything?

Judge: Gilad, what did I say about interrupting?

Gilad: Sorry, sorry! It won't happen again.

17

Judge: I have made my decision.

Gilad: Guilty, of course! Throw them in jail!

Judge: Gilad, I am tempted to throw you in jail! Will you listen to my judgement?

Gilad: Yes, of course, Judge.

Judge: I believe these brothers are not thieves. They are simply very good at seeing things that the rest of us miss. In fact, I would like to use their skills in future cases. I'm sure together we can catch many thieves!

Tazim: Thank you, sir!

Latif: We would be happy to work with you.

Sadiq: It would be an honour, sir.

Kamran: Thank you for believing us.

Gilad: But what about my camel?
If they didn't steal it, where can it be?

Judge: I am certain these four brothers
can help you find your camel. They have
great skill when it comes to tracking
animals. I only hope they will forgive you
for accusing them of theft.

Tazim: We would be happy to help you, Gilad.

Kamran: I'm sure your camel can't be too far away.
It's lame, after all.

Sadiq: Don't worry, we'll find it.

Latif: Let's go back to the path where we met.
That is a good place to start.

Judge: The four brothers and Gilad returned
to the dusty path where they first met.

21

Tazim: Look! Here are more camel footprints leading off the path. It must have wandered this way.

Kamran: And here is a broken branch where the camel must have brushed past. Look, there's a tuft of fur it left behind.

Sadiq: I think the camel went down this slope. Let's follow and see where the footprints lead.

Latif: I can see a grove of trees. And what is that just behind a tree trunk?

Gilad: My camel!

Judge: The four brothers led Gilad down
a sandy slope towards a small grove
of palm trees. And sure enough, there was
his camel resting in the cool shade.

Gilad: Thank you, brothers! Please forgive me,
and accept this jar of honey
as a gift of thanks.

Four Clever Brothers 🖋 Lynne Rickards

Teaching notes written by Sue Bodman and Glen Franklin

Using this book

Content/theme/subject

This playscript is designed to be read aloud during guided reading lessons. Each member of a group of six has a speaking part. The story follows a traditional style of retelling in which the wise brothers are able to prove to the judge that they are not thieves, and can help the camel owner recover his lost camel. Other traditional tales, such as Grimms' 'Four Skilful Brothers', or more recent versions, such as 'The Three Brothers' by JK Rowling, can offer opportunities for comparison.

Language structure

- Easily recognisable stylistic use of traditional language, such as: 'Tell me …' on p.8 and 'Hear my plea!' on p.13.

- Sentences may have two or three clauses and a greater range of connectives (for example, on p.20).

Book structure/visual features

- Some conventions of a playscript are followed, e.g. cast list, stage directions, dialogue layout.

- Clear layout of direct speech supports expression when reading aloud.

Vocabulary and comprehension

- Developing comprehension is supported through speech layout and punctuation.

- Statements, questions and exclamations are used to demonstrate the meaning effectively, and to uphold the stylistic devices, such as 'Tell me, is your camel blind in one eye?' on p.8.

Curriculum links

Science – Use non-fiction sources to explore different animal tracks. Look for evidence of animal or bird tracks in the local area. Make animal tracks in sand and clay for other children to guess the animal.

Geography – Explore how real-life camels are used to support life in desert regions. The Cambridge Reading Adventure book 'A World of Deserts' (Gold Band) might be useful here.

Learning outcomes

Children can:

- recognise features of playscripts and comment on their effectiveness

- use the grammar and language structure to support the decoding of longer or less familiar words

- monitor the effectiveness of oral reading in conveying meaning to the listener.

Planning for guided reading

Lesson One To identify the features of playscripts and comment on effectiveness

Children may be unfamiliar with the use of playscripts in guided reading. Explain that in this lesson, they will each be allocated a part, and will read as if they are the character. Turn to the cast list (p.2-3). Explain its function and explore the layout, noting how each character's name is written in bold, and there is a little description of each. Ask the children if there are any words they do not understand (for example' 'justice' or 'honour'). Give a brief overview of the story: In this play, Gilead has lost his camel. He thinks the four brothers have stolen it, and he takes them to the judge.

Say: In a play, it is important that you read clearly and take notice of the punctuation to help you sound like you are talking. Go to p.7, for example, where Gilad is first introduced. Look at the use of punctuation, short sentence structure and expressive language ('Help! You there!') indicating how this should be said. Have each child practise this speech, and listen to each other to